T0318041

RUTH HALEY
BARTON

• •

SABBATH

JOURNAL

• • •

What Your Soul
Wants to Say
to God

An imprint of InterVarsity Press
Downers Grove, Illinois

InterVarsity Press
P.O. Box 1400 | Downers Grove, IL 60515-1426
ivpress.com | email@ivpress.com

©2023 by Ruth Haley Barton

All rights reserved. No part of this book may be reproduced in any form without written permission from InterVarsity Press.

InterVarsity Press® is the publishing division of InterVarsity Christian Fellowship/USA®. For more information, visit intervarsity.org.

While any stories in this book are true, some names and identifying information may have been changed to protect the privacy of individuals.

The publisher cannot verify the accuracy or functionality of website URLs used in this book beyond the date of publication.

Cover design and image composite: David Fassett

Interior design: Daniel van Loon

ISBN 978-1-5140-0677-1 (print)

Printed in the United States of America ∞

Library of Congress Cataloging-in-Publication Data
A catalog record for this book is available from the Library of Congress.

30 29 28 27 26 25 24 23 | 13 12 11 10 9 8 7 6 5 4 3 2 1

Welcome!

Every spiritual practice corresponds to some deep desire of the human heart, and sabbath-keeping is no exception. God's gift of the sabbath corresponds to our desire for rest . . . replenishment . . . freedom . . . delight . . . a way of life that works. The commitment to embrace a sabbath practice (rather than just reading and dreaming about it) emerges from a deep connection with our own souls and the desires that stir there.

Authentic desire is the only motivation powerful enough to help us establish and maintain this countercultural rhythm. This journal is meant to be a place where you can interact honestly and freely with God about your longing for a way of life that works: one that is grounded in life-giving rhythms of work and rest. It will keep bringing you back to your desire so that desire can deepen into intent, until eventually you are ordering your life in new ways.

With quotations drawn from *Embracing Rhythms of Work and Rest*, this journal provides space for you to respond to the reflection questions found in the

"What Your Soul Wants to Say to God" section at the end of each chapter. What you write here does not have to be profound; it just needs to be true. And even after you have finished reading the book, you can keep using this journal as a sacred space to say something true to God as part of your sabbath practice.

You will find blank pages intermixed with lined pages to give you space to draw or simply write outside the lines. Also included to use as you wish are fifty-two "Sabbath Prompts" to spark your practice and give shape to your sabbath journey. We have placed this list at the back of the journal in order to encourage you to use these ideas as is fitting for the needs of your soul and not as a checklist.

I am not saying everyone must write in a journal as part of their sabbath practice. All I know is that when I am able to express something true to God on the sabbath, something inexplicably restful happens. Rather than staying stuck in the wearying pattern of holding everything in and holding myself tight, journaling offers a way to open up and invite God in. This is a unique kind of rest for the soul.

If journaling ever starts to feel like work to you or seems like a burden, don't do it. But if the idea of journaling once a week as part of your sabbath practice feels fresh, inviting, or helpful—by all means, give it a try and see what God does with it!

To my knowledge God has never "taken back" the gift of the sabbath—it was one of the Ten Commandments, after all, and the best one if you ask me!

Sabbath-keeping is a way of ordering all of life around the pattern of working six days and ceasing on the seventh. It helps us arrange our lives to honor the rhythms of work and rest, fruitfulness and dormancy, giving and receiving, being and doing, activism and surrender.

Sabbath is one of God's greatest gifts to us in our humanity . . .
it is both beautiful and functional, luxurious and
essential all at the same time.

Sabbath-keeping is not primarily a private discipline. It is and always has been a discipline to be entered into with those closest to us.

The only way to even begin taking steps toward a sabbath practice is to let yourself fall in love with this day so that you long for it as you would long for a loved one.

Sabbath is more than a lifestyle suggestion . . . it is a spiritual precept that emerges from God's very nature.

What if rest has already been created and all I have to do is find ways to participate? What if God has already done the work of creating this sanctuary in time and all I have to do is enter in?

To experience ourselves cherished for who we are while not achieving anything or doing anything to earn the air we breathe is a revelation each and every sabbath.

Sabbath is first and foremost about the freedom to live our lives on God's own terms for us rather than living in bondage to anyone, anything, or any culture.

One day a week we practice trusting God as our ultimate strength and provider rather than putting all our faith in what we can secure for ourselves through our 24-7 striving.

One of the main functions of sabbath-keeping is to give us a regular, built-in opportunity for remembering who we are and to whom we belong. No matter how enslaved we've been during the week, on the sabbath we remember our true identity as free people.

To practice sabbath, we need to know what we are in bondage to—what has us in its grip—and that is precisely the thing we should cease.

Sabbath-keeping is a communal discipline that needs to be led and practiced in community.

When we invite people to join us in Christian community, what are we inviting them into? A life of Christian busyness or a way of life that works?

*To fully understand and practice sabbath-keeping, we must
see it as integrally connected with trust——that is, an increasing
capacity to trust God for provision and for our very lives.*

Sabbath-keeping and other aspects of self-care are not merely self-indulgent luxuries; they are part and parcel of healthy leadership that is sustainable for the long haul. It is what gives us an authentic platform from which to teach and guide others.

Technological advances have become a source of the deepest kind of exhaustion, foisted on us in the most manipulative ways by those who do not have our best interests at heart.

There are many symptoms and sources of exhaustion these days, but one of the deepest and most pernicious is that constant stimulation that comes from being plugged in, stirred up, and constantly promoting ourselves.

It is nearly impossible to live sabbath rhythms well and consistently if the communities we are a part of don't support them and if they are not led intentionally.

In a sabbath state of mind, as we are being resuscitated by God's gift of rest, we may have enough capacity to take an interest in others and enjoy them rather than being so focused on hoarding our time and energy.

Eventually, gratitude turns into delight as we engage life's simple pleasures from a more rested place—especially those gifts and pleasures that can't be bought and marketed in a consumeristic culture.

Sabbath offers a deep kind of replenishment and re-membering—that is, giving God the opportunity to mend our tattered lives and put us back together again in the way only God can.

Sabbath is a gift for all ages and stages, but it will be experienced differently throughout the various seasons of our lives. It is good to be open to this rather than getting stuck in assuming sabbath will look the same in every season.

When we practice sabbath in such a way that our family is not able to engage in it with us, we are missing one of the basic intentions of the practice: families and communities resting together and being shaped together by the freedom, the faith, and the goodness of what God has for us.

Sabbath is a means of grace—a way of opening to the transforming work of God beyond anything we can accomplish for ourselves.

One of the main things we are freed for on the sabbath is to simply be human—to honor the body's need for rest, the spirit's need for replenishment, and the soul's need to delight itself in God for God's own sake.

Our resistance and/or our dismissive attitude toward sabbath is often related to an unwillingness to acknowledge and live within the limits of our humanity, to honor our finiteness, to confront the nasty lie that we are indispensable.

Sabbath shows us how to move beyond lamenting our limits as liabilities to embracing them as gifts that are part and parcel of being human—an aspect of our created selves that God intended and called good.

Sabbath-keeping will mess with us, not just as individuals but as communities!

On the sabbath we encounter the God who has been waiting for us—waiting to be gracious to us and show mercy to us—in ways we cannot always fully perceive.

Sabbath Prompts

1. What has been your history with sabbath? Get in touch with your experience of sabbath—its presence, its absence, how it was taught and/or practiced (if it was taught and/or practiced), how it was avoided, and how this history has shaped your current attitude about sabbath.

2. Is there anything happening in your life right now that is stopping you in your tracks or waking you up to your limits and longings for sane rhythms of work and rest? Create some space to pay attention to what your soul wants to say to God about what you are experiencing, and maybe even express it in words, prayer, art, or music.

3. Reflect on the rhythms found in the natural world: the seasons, waves and tides, night and day, rhythms of your heartbeat and breathing, waking and sleeping, eating three meals a day, music, and so on. Which of these rhythms is most inviting and compelling to you as you think about the goodness and necessity of sabbath rhythms? Allow these images to draw you into fresh thoughts or feelings about the gift of sabbath.

4. Think back on a day that for you was the perfect day. What aspects or components of that day made it so good? What would it be like to think about having a day like that once a week?

5. What feels uncomfortable or impossible to you about sabbath-keeping? Say something honest to God about that.

6. Who do you share life with, and what is it like to think of sharing sabbath with them?

7. If you have ever been in love or imagined being in love, how might "falling in love" with the sabbath be something like falling in love with a person? What would it take for you to fall in love with the sabbath?

8. Jot down some thoughts about aspects of life in our culture (generally) and your life (specifically) that make embracing sane rhythms of work and rest seem difficult or even impossible. Do not try to solve anything or fix anything yet; just be with God with this sense of difficulty and any emotions surrounding it.

9. Trace the theme of sabbath and rest throughout Scripture, using a special colored pen to highlight words and phrases that speak to you about this important pattern. You can start with these key passages or use a concordance or a Bible app to uncover more: Genesis 1:31–2:3; Exodus 16 (entire chapter); Exodus 18:17-18, 22-23; Exodus 20:8-11; Exodus 23:10-13; Exodus 31:12-18; Exodus 34:21; Deuteronomy 5:12-15; Joshua 1:13-15; 1 Kings 8:56; Psalm 116:7; Isaiah 14:7; Isaiah 30:15; Jeremiah 6:16; Matthew 11:28-30; Matthew 12:6-8, 11-12; Mark 2:23-27; Hebrews 4:4-11.

10. Take time to consider that sabbath is more than a lifestyle suggestion, but rather it's a spiritual precept that emerges from the very nature of God. Do you agree or disagree? What does this mean to you?

11. Make a list of all your reasons for not practicing sabbath—even those that seem silly or embarrassing. Share your resistance to sabbath with God and listen for God's response.

12. When do you experience the privilege of partnering with God in the context of your work? Does this happen often, rarely, sometimes? How might you expand this sense of partnering with God when you're working and resting with God when you're resting?

13. Is there any area in your life right now where you recognize you are in bondage—where you're not free to live on God's best terms for you? What might it look like for you to resist bondage and practice freedom in this area one day a week? Consider bringing this up as a conversation topic with a spiritual friend and ask them to pray for you as you process this awareness.

14. How do you react/respond to the concept of "sabbath as resistance"? Is this a new idea for you? Is it energizing? Frightening? Uncomfortable? Recognizing fear or discomfort can offer you the option of deciding to push through it rather than allowing fear to become an obstacle. If this idea is energizing, you can tap into that and use it as motivation.

15. Many people are thinking about sabbath these days and trying to practice it, but typically they think of it as a personal issue they are trying to figure out for themselves, by themselves. Reflect on the idea that sabbath is intended to be a *communal* discipline. How does this shift the way you think about sabbath?

16. With whom would you like to share a sabbath practice? Who might be willing to explore this practice with you?

17. If you worship within a faith community, reflect on how your community helps or hinders your practice of sabbath. If you are on a path toward embracing a sabbath practice, what could your community do to help? Is there anyone in your community you could talk to about this?

18. When you think of inviting someone to join your church community, what are you inviting them into—really? A life of Christian busyness or a way of life that works? Be as honest as you can about this.

19. If you are a leader in your community, what is your life modeling for others as it has to do with finding a way of life that works?

20. In what areas of your life would you need to trust God more completely in order to embrace a sabbath practice? Can you envision how practicing sabbath might form deeper levels of trust in you?

21. Do you know any sabbath leaders who are practicing life-giving rhythms of work and rest and thus are able to provide leadership for others from a place of integrity and authenticity? What does their way of life stir in you?

22. *Embracing Rhythms of Work and Rest* highlights a new kind of bondage: our addiction to technology (chapter five). Take some time to conduct a "fearless moral inventory" of your relationship with technology. Are you "free" in relation to technology, or is there any way in which you experience yourself to be in bondage?

23. Consider unplugging from technology as part of your next sabbath. What plans need to be made ahead of time? Who do you need to communicate with and what arrangements need to be made with them? Think through any materials (such as directions, etc.) that need to be printed ahead of time, reservations that need to be made (if you are planning an activity), and getting groceries and other needed items into the house so you do not need to rely on technology for anything on this day.

24. How badly do you want to rest the part of you that is overstimulated from always being plugged in and "on"? Give yourself time to get in touch with your desire because this will be essential in any attempt to add this countercultural move to your sabbath practice.

25. How would you describe the feeling of delight? Take time to reflect on moments or occasions in your life when you experienced pleasure and delight.

26. Make a list of things that delight you—everything from things that seem trivial and not worth mentioning (like putzing around your yard, straightening up your desk or tool bench, talking a nap in the sun, fishing even if you don't catch anything, or going for a slow walk without a destination) to those that seem a little more obvious (writing poetry or listening to music, reading for pleasure, enjoying the unhurried process of cooking a special meal, going to a concert or a play, going on a long run, or playing with children, grandchildren, nieces, or nephews). Keep adding to the list as you pay more and more attention to experiences that bring you delight.

27. Let yourself dream about a day that is made up of moments that delight you. Brainstorm how you can incorporate more delight into your sabbath, noticing how it feels to even consider this.

28. Who are the people you love and would enjoy most on the sabbath? Have a brainstorming session about how you can share sabbath meaningfully together.

29. Is there a neighbor or someone in your community who is in need of kindness? Extend kindness in a way that does not feel like work.

30. Tilden Edwards makes the point that "corporate worship can be the pinnacle of Christian sabbath, but it is not the sabbath." (See chapter six in *Embracing Rhythms of Work and Rest* for the full quote.) What does this mean to you? How might the commitment to sabbath rest affect the way your community worships together and plans for Sundays?

31. Reflect with God on your current season of life. What unique challenges and opportunities related to sabbath-keeping are present in this season? Speak to God about these things, and then listen to what God has to say in response. Take a look at chapter seven of *Embracing Rhythms of Work and Rest* to see if any of the ideas offered there correspond to the challenges and opportunities of the season in which you find yourself.

32. Let go of heavy expectations about perfection and determine to work positively and creatively with the life God has given you. Since God is the one who has bestowed the gift of sabbath, seek God on this matter and trust God to help you find your way to meaningful and regular rest even during this season.

33. Rabbi Abraham Heschel in his book *The Sabbath* says that sabbath "is not a day to shoot fireworks or to turn somersaults, but an opportunity to mend our tattered lives." Is there anything that feels tattered in your life right now? Do you have any idea what it might look like to experience sabbath as an opportunity for mending that tattered place versus creating more stimulation?

34. Is there a hard thing you have been working hard to hold in and manage? Create space on the sabbath to rest with it instead—journal about it, talk about it with someone you trust, cry the tears you have been holding back, or find some other way to be with God with it. Trust God with this tender part of yourself and see how God meets you.

35. Find some time and inner space to reflect on the reality of limits. How do you relate to the idea that to be human is to have limits, and how do you relate to your own limits? Do you ignore them? Are you embarrassed by them? Do you insist on behaving like you do not have limits? How far back does this pattern go, and where does it come from?

36. How do you respond to the idea that there is something deeply spiritual about honoring the limits of our existence as human beings? When have you experienced "a spirituality of limits" (chapter eight of *Embracing Rhythms of Work and Rest*) or witnessed it in someone else?

37. Do you have any boundaries between your work life and your personal life? Describe them. Are these boundaries enough? Are there any additional boundaries you could put in place in order to protect a sabbath state of being?

38. What are you willing to say no to in order to say yes to the gift of sabbath? As you feel ready, make specific and concrete plans around eliminating work, buying and selling, worry and other mental stressors, and technology during your sabbath time.

39. How would you describe life in your body these days? Draw a picture if that is easier! What would it be like to have one day a week when you choose activities that are restful and replenishing to your body rather than driving your body like a truck? Listen to your body and then, on the sabbath, choose only activities that rest your body and feel good in your body.

40. From your list of things that delight you (question twenty-six) choose an activity or two that seem restful for your mind and replenishing to your spirit. Incorporate these into your sabbath today.

41. Take some time to journal about things you are grateful for from the past week. Thank God for them and allow gratitude and joy to fill your heart and energize your spirit.

42. Notice how your soul feels drawn to be with God today, whether it's through silence or prayer with words, reflecting on a Scripture

passage that stood out to you this week, doing an extended examen of the past week and inviting God to show you where God was present and where God felt absent, reading a spiritual book, taking a nature walk or a mountain hike—and then choose it!

43. Consider if there is a simple ritual that would help you (and those you are practicing with) to begin and end your sabbath in a meaningful way, and then try it!

44. If you are a leader in a church or community, consider what you are modeling for others. As they observe your life, do you think they see a life of Christian busyness or a way of life that works? If you are feeling brave, you might ask a few people in your community how they are observing your way of life and then listen carefully.

45. Once you have established the inner authority that comes from your own practice, identify one thing you could do to begin cultivating a sabbath community. See chapter nine of *Embracing Rhythms of Work and Rest* for ideas.

46. Does your church or ministry organization have a sabbatical policy (an extended time of rest and replenishment every seventh year) in place for pastors and ministry leaders as one aspect of being a sabbath community? If not, what would it take to begin considering this?

47. In the quiet of sabbath time, reflect on God's words to the people of Israel in Isaiah 30. What obstacles and resistances to sabbath rest do you note in this passage? Which ones resonate with your own experience? Speak honestly to God about whatever it is that prevents you from embracing these God-ordained rhythms of work and rest.

48. We often think of ourselves as waiting on God, but in Isaiah 30 we are introduced to a God who waits for us—a God who waits to be gracious to us and show mercy to us if we would simply choose the rest God is offering. What does it mean to you to know that God is waiting for you? How do you respond?

49. The phrase "in returning and rest you shall be saved" (Isaiah 30:15 NRSV) seems to indicate a pattern, not just a random and haphazard approach to resting. How might regular rhythms of work and rest actually save you?

50. What do you hope might get formed in you through the practice of sabbath? What hope does the possibility of ordering your life around sabbath rhythms foster within you?

51. Establishing a sabbath practice is so countercultural that it will require support and a safe place to process your experiences. Discern whom you might like to have ongoing conversations with about the sabbath, and then ask them! The worst they can do is say no. A conversation guide is provided just after appendix B in the back of *Embracing Rhythms of Work and Rest*.

52. Do something before you do everything! Identify one day in the future when you (and your family, if you are practicing with family) can take a sabbath. Using the sabbath instructions contained in appendix A of *Embracing Rhythms of Work and Rest*, identify one or two ideas you want to try and that you think might go well for yourself and anyone else involved. Try taking a sabbath day once and see what happens. Let God guide you from there!

ALSO BY
Ruth Haley Barton

Embracing Rhythms of Work and Rest

Invitation to Retreat

Invitation to Solitude and Silence

Life Together in Christ

Longing for More

Pursuing God's Will Together

Sacred Rhythms

Strengthening the Soul of Your Leadership

**For more information about the work of the
Transforming Center, please visit
www.transformingcenter.org.**